JOIE DE VIVRE

Savoring the Joy of Life at the Modern Table

Happy Valentine's Day

Thanks ♡

02/14/19

BOUCHERIE

Written by Jessica Colley Clarke

Photography by Ian Gittler

Image on page 4 © Jean Marquis / BHVP / Roger-Viollet / The Image Works

Image on page 6 © Daniel Frasnay / Akg-images / The Image Works

Image on page 8 © Roger-Viollet/The Image Works

Image on page 9 © Gaston Paris / Roger-Viollet / The Image Works

Image on page 11 © Akg-images / Paul Almasy / The Image Works

Image on page 63 © Jai Nima Idowu

Image on page 66 © Jai Nima Idowu

Designed by Savvy Studio

Produced by Tijana Masic

1st edition of 5,000 copies

Printed in Rhode Island, USA

ISBN 978-1-5323-5554-7

CONTENTS

FOREWORD

Welcome to Joie de Vivre

Joie de vivre can be found during a quiet morning spent solo with a newspaper, a relaxed lunch with an old friend, or a drink on your walk home from work. Our everyday routines have potential for moments of joy, if we choose to stop and recognize them. Once we start, we may begin to notice that these moments present themselves more frequently.

When you make the time to garden or go for long walks or listen to music, you are finding the potential for satisfaction in the every day. *Joie de vivre* is about savoring small moments of pleasure, devoting time to building relationships, and saying yes to dessert.

Anticipation is entangled with *joie de vivre*. Part of any pleasure is the thought of it beforehand. Walking to the boulangerie, we think about the first bite of a croissant warm from the oven. The present act is connected to every croissant memory we can recall. Certain foods and cities and streets have a power over us—they make us happy just thinking of them.

This philosophy is built on an absence of guilt, a belief that we deserve pleasure in the everyday, and an appreciation of beauty and refined taste. *Joie de vivre* likes company, but doesn't require it.

Our strongest relationships are built over meals when we break bread, pour wine, and listen to our appetites. At Boucherie, we believe that life is lived around the table. This book will give you a glimpse at where we come from, what we value, and what is on top of our table.

Santé!

BELLE EPOQUE

"Paris is always a good idea."

Audrey Hepburn

Belle Epoque Parisians valued pleasure:
passions were to be explored, conversation
should be animated, and Champagne coupes
should never be empty.

During *Belle Epoque*, artists and writers worked by day and caroused by night, filling Paris cafés with music and conversation. During this decadent period (between wars from 1871 to 1914), *joie de vivre* was the defining philosophy of the era.

Belle Epoque, especially at the turn of the century, is given credit for French cuisine gaining esteem. At the Hotel Ritz Paris, Head Chef Auguste Escoffier created a posh gathering place. A focus on food fit right in with the era's obsessions with beauty, pleasure, and entertainment.

BELLE
EPOQUE
POSTERS

Colorful, evocative posters were a signature artistic accent of Belle Epoque. During this period, the status of advertising posters was elevated to a fine art for the first time.

Boucherie continues this tradition with a significant collection of original posters from the era, including ornate, playful advertisements for the liquid muse of Belle Epoque, absinthe.

In addition to food and drink, this era is also known for entertainment. Music halls, cabaret, and masked balls were all popular at the time. After the war, the mood was light hearted and an attitude of positivity and euphoria was palpable in the Paris streets.

At Boucherie, we set out to capture some of the carefree spirit of *Belle Epoque*. The bar is stocked with absinthe, an often-noted muse of the era. Sidewalk tables are in a prime position for people watching and our menu contains touches of decadence from foie gras to crème brulee.

The philosophy of this era inspired the foundation of Boucherie. Each day and evening, we set the table for a carefree meal with family and friends. Fashions, centuries, and technology may be different, but the spirit is the same.

SETTING THE SCENE

"Anything can happen at any time."

Joseph Goldstein

Atmosphere is an essential piece of the joie
de vivre puzzle. Countless tiny details—from
lighting to music to design—add up to create
ambience. Boucherie is inspired by the comfort
and camaraderie of traditional brasseries but
is firmly rooted in the pleasures of today.

Sit down at a bar and the moment is full of possibility. By the time your glass is empty, you may connect with a stranger over anything from travel to music to a similar family saga. In a diverse city like New York, a dynamic interaction is only a drink order away.

Connection is at the heart of *joie de vivre*. Something happens when people of different ages and cultures mix in a place that encourages interaction. The traditional brasserie is designed to make everyone feel welcome; it is a timeless, any-hour-of-the-day space where people of all backgrounds and interests can gather. It is the right fit for moments of the day ranging from morning coffee to an after dinner nightcap.

The Town Square

The old world town square is a
community gathering place. People know
from experience that they can come, sit, and
over the course of a coffee or a newspaper,
they will encounter neighbors and friends.
The design of Boucherie incorporates a town
square of bistro tables, where neighbors come
to mingle, eat, and drink in a comfortable
space with plentiful natural light.

The Butcher Counter

For meat lovers, the main stage of Boucherie is the butcher counter, where all steaks are grilled over open flames. In this interactive space, guests can talk with the chef as their meal is prepared. Cooking advice is shared and guests chat with their neighbors as meat is grilled over cherry oak embers.

The Communal Table

Large gatherings and lively conversation were a staple of *Belle Epoque*. Communal tables offer a space for multi-generational dinners or large celebrations with friends. Inspired by family feasts, the communal table at Boucherie gives the home cook a night off and leaves the meal preparation to a chef.

The Bar

Long bars are a symbol of traditional French brasseries. During *Belle Epoque*, Parisians filled the pewter bar with glasses of absinthe and Champagne. This ritual continues a century later with the bar at Boucherie. Over a cocktail, conversations are sparked between friends and strangers.

The Gallery

Within an old world town square, there's usually a spot for intimate conversations that is away from the main bustle, but still has a view of the action. The equivalent at Boucherie is the gallery, where couples and friends gather at tables with a touch of privacy. The theater of the evening unfolds around this space.

The Sounds of Boucherie

Paris was not only a creative hub for artists and writers, but also for musicians. Audiences were hungry for entertainment and musicians found creative and individual freedom in the City of Light, capturing the spirit of this place and moment in time. The music at Boucherie includes both the sounds of Paris and musicians who were inspired by the city.

1. Lionel Hampton All Stars - Stardust
2. Mademoiselle de Paris - André Claveau
3. Jean Sablon - Ces Petites Choses
4. Ne me quitte pas - Jacques Brel
5. Night and day - feat. Jo Duval et son orchestre
6. Ni toi ni moi - Joséphine Baker
7. C'est Si Bon - Eartha Kitt
8. Je Cherche Un Homme - Eartha Kitt
9. April In Paris (1956) - Billie Holiday
10. Le Claqueur de Doigts - Serge Gainsbourg
11. Cheek to Cheek - Ella & Louis
12. April In Paris - Charlie Parker
13. I'm In the Mood for Love - James Moody
14. Une Petite Laitue - Roy Eldridge
15. Summertime - Chet Baker Quartet
16. I Love Paris - Coleman Hawkins
17. Tout doux, tout doucement - Marcel Amont
18. Say It With a Kiss - Artie Shaw and His Orchestra

The Patio

Fresh air adds another layer to a dining experience. Herbs and plants from lavender to thyme lend a fragrant touch to Boucherie's seasonal patio. Inspired by the countryside in the south of France, the patio is a generous sidewalk space with bistro tables among vintage containers overflowing with rosemary and oregano. On warm summer nights, the buzz of the restaurant flows out into the street.

THROUGHOUT THE DAY

"Heaven to be the first one up and to eat breakfast all alone."

Katharine Hepburn

The French don't wait for the weekend to live their lives. They also don't wait for the evenings, but create moments of pleasure throughout the day. This is the essence of joie de vivre: making it a priority to find moments of joy.

In Paris, the morning is full of life. Bakeries are buzzing, sidewalk tables are full of locals drinking coffee and reading the newspaper, and shops are opening for the day. While in some cities, restaurants remain dark until the dinner hour, many restaurants in France open early and close late, maximizing the opportunity for a little *joie de vivre*.

There is a certain joy to a lively, candlelit restaurant in the evening, but there are other pleasures to be found throughout the day. You may love the quiet of the morning, with the aroma of freshly ground coffee and the temptation of flaky pastries. Others may prefer a late breakfast before the lunch rush, perhaps an omelette and salad with lemony dressing.

With windows open and bright, natural light, a bistro is a pleasant place to linger over lunch. Skip the 20-minute desk lunch and at least sometimes, gather with family or friends for an unhurried meal in the middle of your day.

The slumber of the afternoon has its own appeal: coffee or cocktail? These peaceful hours are perfect for getting lost in a good book or brainstorming with colleagues. If hunger strikes, some *mousse de foie gras* or a simple order of *pommes frites* provide a blast of taste in your afternoon.

The day unfolds into green hour, with refreshing cocktails poured liberally at the bar. During the vibrant heart of the evening, wine glasses are raised, plates of mussels and escargots are passed around the table, and steaks are devoured.

Then the fun of late night begins, with unexpected conversations between tables or people at the bar and final drinks ordered. With flushed cheeks and bellies full, people may not be in a rush to go home, instead savoring a small glass of absinthe while the evening crowd clears.

From first thing in the morning to the final
hours of the night, there's ample opportunity in
a day to experience *joie de vivre* whenever you
find a spare moment. Cross our threshold, and
you will find an environment for adding more
satisfaction into life's little moments.

BREAD
AND BUTTER

"Good bread is the most fundamentally satisfying of all foods; and
good bread with fresh butter, the greatest of all feasts."

James Beard

Simple pleasures often provide the most satisfaction. But for simple to be stellar, the details are important. After all, it's quality, and not quantity that defines the French table.

Every morning, while the rest of us are asleep in our beds, the bakers are at work. Before sunrise, they are calculating exact proportions of flour, salt, yeast, and water to produce superior bread. They utilize years of experience, knowing from touch and each day's weather conditions exactly what the dough needs. From their pre-dawn labor, we are given one of life's treasured morning rituals: bread still warm from the oven.

The French are not carb shy; they are a strong example of how to find a balanced and guilt-free place for bread on your table. A visit to the boulangerie for flaky croissants, a baguette, or maybe a *pain au chocolat* is routine. Breakfast often makes use of yesterday's leftover baguette, toasted and simply topped with butter and jam. Alongside a strong coffee, it makes for an easy and satisfying morning meal.

INTRODUCTION TO FRENCH BUTTER

To make butter, fresh cream is churned to separate buttermilk and butterfat. While this process is quite simple, there are many other factors that contribute to the final product.

At Boucherie, our butter contains 86% butterfat; milk comes from family farms in Vermont and is all-natural with no growth hormones.

Beyond breakfast, bread makes an appearance throughout the day in the French diet. A lunchtime picnic may include a crunchy baguette split, spread with butter, and filled with a couple slices of premium ham and cheese. Dinner around the family table may include a loaf set on top of a well-worn cutting board, with each person tearing a hunk of bread from the loaf according to their appetite.

Even the best loaf of bread would be incomplete without the right butter.

In France, bread baking is often left to the professionals. Even the most accomplished home cooks typically leave the baguette shaping and pastry making to the experts. At Boucherie, we feature the work of some of New York's most accomplished bakers. These artisanal breads are the perfect accompaniment to the cheese, foie gras, steak tartare, and mussels that fill our menu.

If *joie de vivre* were to be distilled down into a single bite, it would likely be a piece of baguette generously spread with butter.

FRIDAY

la Grenobloise

SATURDAY

Bourguignon

THE CLASSICS

"Tell me what you eat and I'll tell you what you are."

Jean Anthelme Brillat-Savarin

Some of our most ordered dishes are straight up French classics. These familiar favorites satisfy every time, from silky foie gras to a perfectly grilled rib-eye.

Everyone has a favorite onion soup memory. A bowl of *soupe à l'oignon gratinée* can bring back flashes of late lunches in Paris bistros or snowstorms at home with onions slowly caramelizing on the stovetop. When we eat soulful food, the scents, setting, and company all burrow down deep in our memory. Our past pleasure becomes part of our future satisfaction.

Our classics all have one thing in common: time. These are slow cooked dishes, where flavor is the result of patience. To achieve a superior taste, you can't be in a rush. We must slow down, adjust to the pace that a dish dictates, until after hours or even days of waiting, *voilà*, the dish is finally ready to serve.

"The first thing I do when I arrive in the morning is look for the wine. Is the wine there? The butter? The shallots? French cuisine is all about wine and butter. If you don't have these ingredients, you can't start cooking."

– JEROME DIHUI, *Executive Chef*

Jerome Dihui

Boucherie's Executive Chef Jerome Dihui grew up in the Ivory Coast where his mother had a small restaurant. School was conducted in French and time spent outside of school was either at the market, his mother's restaurant, or the neighborhood boulangerie.

After moving to the U.S. in 1991, Jerome cooked at several of New York's most acclaimed French restaurants, including 14 years at Pastis in the Meatpacking District.

If you walk by the kitchen at Boucherie, you're likely to see Jerome presiding over these dishes down to their final detail. Here, he shares tips and recipes for our most popular French classic dishes.

SOUPE à L'OIGNON GRATINÉE

Classic onion soup
Wine pairing recommendation: Pinot Gris from Alsace

"We start by slowly caramelizing Vidalia onions. Then we deglaze the pot with red wine and a bit of red port—it gives a hint of sweetness and a rich color. Next comes the veal stock and the herbs (thyme, bay leaf, and fennel seed). For serving, we ladle the soup into a crock, top it with a few slices of baguette and gruyere, and pop it in the oven. When the cheese is bubbling, it gets a final sprinkle of basil and is ready to be served." -J.D.

VEAL STOCK SECRETS

The soul of any bowl of onion soup is the veal stock. At Boucherie, the veal stock cooks slowly for five days before it's ready to be used.

Here are Chef Jerome's tips for making a rich veal stock at home.

* Source veal bones from the butcher (we love the shank and knuckle).

* Roast the bones in a 400-degree oven for one hour.

* While bones are roasting, make a mirepoix (sweat diced carrots, celery, and onion in olive oil).

* In a large pot, add the roasted bones, red wine, water, tomato paste, whole garlic, shallots, and fennel.

* Simmer slowly for five days, including overnight, skimming the pot each morning.

* Don't add flour to thicken the stock—time will take care of that.

* After five days, you'll have a thick, dark, meaty stock that can be used as the foundation for many classic French dishes.

INGREDIENTS *Serves 4*

2½ tablespoons unsalted butter, divided
½ tablespoon vegetable oil
5 ounces slab bacon
2½ pounds Vidalia onions, halved lengthwise, peeled, and thinly sliced
½ teaspoon kosher salt
¼ teaspoon freshly ground black pepper
¼ teaspoon granulated sugar
¾ cup dry red wine
¾ cup red Port
6 cups beef broth
5 sprigs thyme
1 bay leaf
Baguette
1 garlic clove, cut in half lengthwise
5 ounces Gruyère cheese, grated or sliced

PREPARATION

1. In a large pot, melt 2½ tablespoons butter over medium heat. Add bacon, oil, and onions; cook onions until softened, stirring occasionally, about 15 minutes. Add salt, pepper, continue to cook, stirring occasionally, until onions are deep golden brown and caramelized (reducing heat slightly if onions seem to be browning too quickly), 35 to 45 minutes more.

2. Add red wine and red Port, then raise heat to high. Cook until almost all liquid has evaporated, 8 to 10 minutes.

3. Tie thyme and bay leaves into a bundle with twine. Add broth and herb bundle to the pot with the onions. Bring to a boil, reduce to a simmer, and cook, uncovered, until broth is thickened and flavorful, 20 to 30 minutes. Taste and adjust seasoning.

4. Cut two 1/2-inch baguette slices for every serving of soup. Place baguette slices on a rimmed baking sheet and toast in oven until crisp and dry but not browned, about 1 minute per side.

5. Place ramekins or oven safe bowls on a rimmed baking sheet, ladle soup on top. Top each serving of soup with toasts and cheese. Bake until cheese is melted and bubbling.

MOUSSE *de* FOIE GRAS

Hudson Valley foie gras, onion compote, and red wine port sauce
Wine pairing recommendation: Gewürztraminer

"In order to get the texture I love, we combine Hudson Valley foie gras with chicken liver. The texture is soft and delicate, not the slightest bit cakey. Then we add flavorful ingredients like brandy, all spice, and pink salt. I ate a lot pâté growing up, and one bite of this foie gras mousse brings back many happy childhood memories." -J.D.

INGREDIENTS *Serves 30*

1 lobe Hudson Valley foie gras (about 1¼ pounds)
¼ pound chicken liver
¼ cup Cognac
3 teaspoons all spice
3 teaspoons pink salt
4 whole eggs
3 teaspoons kosher salt
2 bottles red wine
2 bottles red Port
Country white large torpedo toast
Red onion compote

PREPARATION

1. Put all ingredients in food processor.

2. Process until smooth and add salt and pepper to taste.

3. Pour into ramekin and place it in a bain-marie with water in bottom. Cover tightly and cook for 20 minutes.

4. Let rest for 1 day to allow flavors to fully develop.

5. Serve cold, spread on country torpedo toast with red onion compote.

FROM THE BUTCHER

"Life is too short for diets."

Paul Bocuse

Of all the aromas that arouse hunger,
few are as powerful as meat on the grill.
Catch the scent of meat and smoke and it
may trigger an instant craving.

Part of the pleasure of eating meat is the full sensory experience. It isn't only the taste of the steak itself, but the sound of the meat when it hits the grill. First we light the fire, patiently waiting for the right moment to ensure a perfect sear. Then we resist the temptation to turn the meat too frequently, and watch it cook, fat releasing into embers below.

WHAT IS DRY AGED MEAT?

When your knife slides through a steak with barely any pressure applied, it is most likely dry aged. This technique is all about tenderness—aging meat in a temperature and humidity controlled space results in steaks that are noticeably more tender and flavorful.

Over time, moisture is naturally drawn out from the meat (causing it to lose a significant percentage of its weight). After 30, 40, or even over 100 days of aging, the result is meat with a buttery texture and concentrated flavor.

Tough connective tissue has broken down naturally over time and what's left is a decadent steak. At Boucherie, we grill a bone-in New York strip that has been aged for 45 days.

The French word "Boucherie" translates to "butchery" in English. From a seat at the butcher counter, guests can watch their steaks sizzle on the wood-burning grill. All steaks are cooked to order in the open kitchen, providing an immersive experience among the scents of wood smoke and meat cooking over cherry oak.

VEAL CUTS

Meat lovers may be familiar with several cuts of beef—from rib-eye to filet mignon to hanger steak—but there are just as many cuts of veal that are worth exploring.

Keep an eye out for veal porterhouse, a cut with the tenderloin on one side of the T-shaped bone and strip loin on the other (just like with beef, choose bone-in cuts for extra flavor).

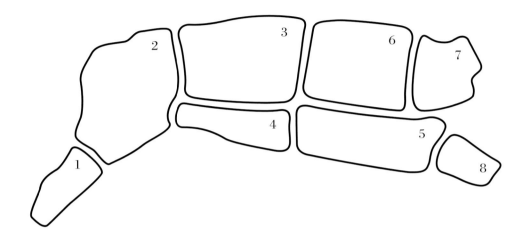

CUTS
LOCATION

1. Hind Shank
2. Bottom Round
3. Loin
4. Flank
5. Breast
6. Ribs
7. Shoulder Roast
8. Foreshank

When we cook with fire, we become part of an ancient tradition of preparing food over flames. But before we can begin cooking, we must source meat of superior quality. A trusted butcher can guide you to the day's best cuts.

For the most flavor, opt for meat on the bone. If you want to experiment with especially tender and flavorful meat, ask your butcher about options for dry aged meats.

CUT OF THE WEEK SERIES

A partnership with Pat LaFrieda Meat Purveyors brings exclusive and unexpected cuts of meat to Boucherie.

Master butcher Pat LaFrieda hand selects cuts of beef, veal, lamb, and pork with limited availability to help meat lovers explore beyond the usual suspects on steakhouse menus.

"Expect cuts from every part of the animal," says Mark Pastore, President and co-owner of Pat LaFrieda Meat Purveyors. "We want to feature every flavor profile and consistency."

The series launched with wagyu sirloin from Snake River Farms, acclaimed for its even marbling and unmatched tenderness.

CÔTE *de* BOEUF
POUR DEUX

40-ounce tomahawk rib-eye, roasted bone marrow
Wine pairing recommendation: A big red from Margaux or Pauillac in Bordeaux

"The bone-in rib-eye has beautiful marbling. It's a
perfect feast for two, especially with a bottle of full-bodied
red wine. We take a great steak to the next level with
roasted bone marrow." -J.D.

INGREDIENTS *Serves 2 to 3 people*

42-ounce Tomahawk ribeye
Bone marrow
Salt
Pepper
4 sprigs of rosemary
4 sprigs of thyme

PREPARATION

1. Remove the rib-eye from the refrigerator and let stand for 1 hour to allow it to come to room temperature.

2. Preheat an oven to 400°F.

3. Drizzle the beef with olive oil, and season all over generously with salt and pepper.

4. Preheat the grill. When the grill is hot, add the rib-eye and cook without moving it, until the meat is well browned on the bottom, 2 to 3 minutes. Turn the meat and grill the other side until well browned, 2 to 3 minutes more. Arrange thyme and rosemary around the meat in an ovenproof sauté pan.

5. Transfer the meat to the oven and roast for 25 minutes (for medium rare). Sprinkle marrow bone with salt and pepper, and roast for 10 minutes.

6. Transfer the rib-eye to a carving board, cover loosely with aluminum foil and let rest for 10 minutes. Then carve the meat from the bone, cutting against the grain into ½ inch slices. Arrange on a warmed platter with the bone marrow and serve immediately.

TASTE OF
THE SEASONS

"Give me juicy autumnal fruit, ripe and red from the orchard."

Walt Whitman

Each month, the market tells us what to eat. From the first sweet asparagus of spring to the ripe, heavy tomatoes of August, the market shows us what produce is at its peak. The French listen to what the market tells them, following the annual cycle of fresh ingredients in their cooking.

Our appetite flows with the seasons—we don't crave the same food on an August afternoon that we do on a chilly January night. At Boucherie, in addition to our classics, we serve a seasonal menu that matches our guests' mood and cravings.

When temperatures are warm in New York City, the French doors swing open and tables flanked by plants, herbs, and flowers fill the sidewalk. This is the season for refreshing cocktails like our Lillet spritz or glasses of icy rosé. Tables are topped with light, flavorful dishes such as our *salade de fruits de mer*, with lump crab and gulf shrimp.

As the season shifts towards fall, New Yorkers are ready to exchange heat and humidity for cool evenings. The fare on our outdoor tables is heartier, as cravings return for roasted chicken over potato puree and steaming bouillabaisse full of shrimp, scallops, mussels, and clams in a saffron broth.

When the heavy coats of winter are pulled from the back of the closet, the patio doors close for the season and our slow cooked dishes take center stage. A rich cassoulet with pork belly, sausage, and white beans or slow-braised *boeuf bourguignon* (our Saturday *spécialité du jour*) are potent cures for any case of the January blues.

Once the snow clears, the first produce of spring is a welcome change from hearty winter fare. Asparagus, artichokes, fava beans, fiddleheads, peas, and new potatoes fill the markets. Salads and soups featuring these fresh ingredients are bright and full of concentrated flavor.

Soon after the markets fill with the tastes of spring, our French doors once again swing open and our sidewalk tables return. Seasonal dishes offer a unique chance at weather-specific *joie de vivre*; don't let summer pass by without raising a glass of cold Sancerre alongside a *salade Niçoise* topped with seared tuna.

SALADE *de* FRUITS *de* MER

Lump crab, gulf shrimp, grapefruit, fennel, celery, and lemon

*The summer menu
at Boucherie is light
and refreshing. Bright
flavors of lemon and
fennel are just right as
a counterpoint to the
season's hot temperatures.*

INGREDIENTS *Serves 2 to 3 people*

25 ounces lump crab meat
1 pound shrimp, peeled, de-veined, and cooked
1 cup shaved fennel
½ cup celery leaves
¼ teaspoon black pepper
¼ cup olive oil
1 grapefruit, peeled and sectioned
Juice of 2 lemons
Kosher salt to taste

PREPARATION

1. In a bowl mix together the shrimp, crab meat, olive oil, lemon juice, and salt.

2. Arrange shaved fennel on a plate, then arrange seafood on top. Top with celery leaves, black pepper, and grapefruit sections. Serve with French bread.

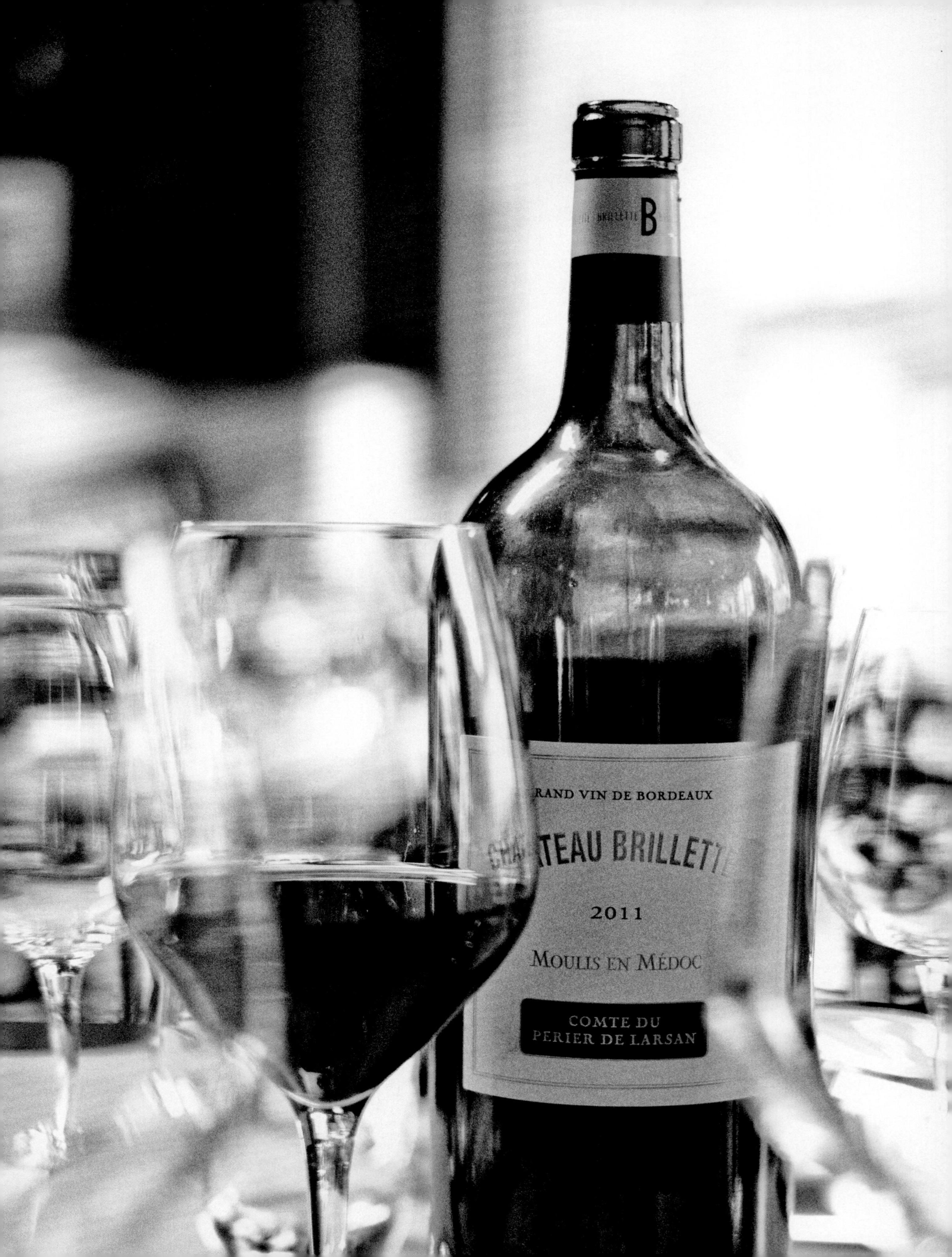
2011
MOULIS EN MÉDOC
COMTE DU
PERIER DE LARSAN

WINE
AND CHEESE

"Drink wine every day, at lunch and dinner,
and the rest will take care of itself."

Waverley Root

Wine and cheese are both elemental components of the French table. Some of our happiest memories begin when we grab a corkscrew—the sound of the popping cork signifies that for now, work has ended and it's time to unwind.

At the French table, wine isn't only for special occasions. It is a regular part of a nourishing meal, often alongside another French staple: cheese. *Fromage* can be a guilt-free part of everyday satisfaction. Finding simple moments of joy in our routines—a glass of wine while we unpack the groceries or a wedge of cheese as an afternoon snack—brings contentment to the everyday.

Once you open that bottle, there are few finer companions than a cheese board. At Boucherie, we add slices of warm baguette to a board of cheese and nuts. It's a marvelously slow way to eat, tearing a piece of baguette and assembling a perfect bite with say, the sharpness of fourme d'ambert blue cheese and a sweet touch of honey. These are tastes that linger in the mouth, that happily play with the nuances of the wine in your glass.

HOW TO
BUILD A
CHEESE BOARD

To build a perfect cheese board, focus on diversity: different textures, cheese from different animals (cow, goat, sheep), and different density.

Choosing cheeses that fit as appetizers or post-dessert is wise for a dinner party; cheese that started out as an appetizer may get nibbled on again towards the end of an evening with a final glass of wine.

Our cheeses:

* Morbier: A semi-soft French cow's milk cheese that is rich and creamy.

* Comté: A semi-hard French cheese with a nutty flavor that is aged in mountain caves.

* Saint-Marcellin: A soft, creamy, cow's milk cheese with an aromatic, runny interior.

* Fourme d'Ambert: A semi-soft farmhouse blue cheese with a sharp and tangy flavor.

* Brebirousse: A creamy French sheep's milk cheese with a notable buttery taste.

* Fleur de Maquis: A semi-soft French sheep's milk cheese with pleasant sour notes.

WINE PAIRING RECOMMENDATIONS FOR A CHEESE BOARD

Boucherie picks for what wine to drink with your cheese board.

If your cheese board is an appetizer:

* Champagne: Fresh, bubbly, and elegant, the high acidity of champagne is a perfect complement to a cheese board.

* Vouvray: Made from Chenin Blanc grapes, this dry white wine is high in acid and minerality with a lovely honey finish.

* Gewürztraminer: Spicy with a great minerality, this low in acid white wine is an ideal counterpoint to a cheese plate.

HOW TO SERVE CHEESE

Don't serve your cheese directly from the refrigerator—very cold cheese lacks the depth of flavor of cheese that has been allowed to come to room temperature.

If your cheese board is a dessert:

* Sauternes: A glass of this chilled sweet dessert wine is a fun match with cheese; it's full-bodied and complex.

* Tawny Port: This fortified wine is ideal with any blue or hard cheese. Hints of dark berries and chocolate are ideal for the end of the night.

* Late harvest Riesling: This complex, fruit forward, rich wine plays well with cheese and is a gorgeous final glass of wine for the evening.

Absinthe

Drip

COCKTAILS
AND ABSINTHE

"When shall we live if not now?"

M.F.K. Fisher

The bar is the heart of any gathering place.
On arrival, you leave the responsibilities of
the day behind for a moment. The first sip of
a finely mixed cocktail is one of life's great
afternoon pleasures.

When the clock struck 5 p.m. in Paris in the 1890s, the city's artists and bohemians had one drink on their mind: absinthe. During *L'Heure Verte*, the green hour, intellectuals and creatives flooded Paris watering holes to discuss the pressing topics of the day and raise a glass of absinthe. The potent, herbal spirit was at the heart of this daily ritual that came to define an era in France.

"New York City doesn't have enough absinthe bars and French based spirits bars. At Boucherie we created a unique list of absinthe and several absinthe-based cocktails, but also shake and stir playful interpretations of classic cocktails with a French twist."

— ANTHONY BOHLINGER

La Fee Verte ("the green fairy") was the drink of choice for writers and artists from Vincent Van Gogh to Oscar Wilde, Pablo Picasso to Ernest Hemingway. But before the poets and painters got their hands on absinthe, it was a medicinal tonic, created by a doctor in Switzerland in the late 18th century. After its heyday, absinthe had a dramatic fall. Rumors about hallucinations and addiction led to its legal ban. Now, almost 100 years later, absinthe is having a renaissance. The herbaceous spirit has shaken off its bad reputation (the mystery surrounding wormwood, a plant that is an ingredient in absinthe, has been solved). Today at Boucherie, absinthe is sipped (see the sidebar on How to Drink Absinthe) and used as an ingredient in cocktails.

How to Drink Absinthe

Absinthe today is typically served one of two ways: as an ingredient in a cocktail, or on its own. Cocktails are a tasty gateway towards learning about the flavors of absinthe, but the best way to experience the spirit is with the ceremony of the traditional absinthe drip.

The bar at Boucherie has several movable absinthe fountains. These fountains slowly drip ice water over a slotted spoon holding a sugar cube that is suspended over a frosted glass of absinthe. Water opens up the flavors and herbal, floral aromas including anise and fennel leap from the glass. As the icy water drips into the glass, there is a change in the color of the absinthe—it morphs from light green to cloudy (this is called the "louche"

effect). Once the sugar cube is dissolved and the ratio of water to absinthe is about 5:1, you stir the mixture and it's ready to drink. Historically, in France, the glass of absinthe was served on a plate. Your tab at the end of the evening? As many plates as you had stacked in front of you.

Absinthe expert and award-winning bartender Anthony Bohlinger is the creative mind behind the cocktail list at Boucherie. Anthony immersed himself in all things absinthe at Brooklyn's Maison Premiere, winner of a James Beard Award for best bar program 2016. Here, he shares details on Boucherie's cocktails.

In addition to absinthe-based drinks, cocktails are at the heart of *joie de vivre* at Boucherie. Classic cocktails, ranging from clean to spirit-forward, often have a French twist. Whether it's Sunday brunch or Tuesday green hour, our bartenders are shaking and stirring drinks that can provide a little escape from your routine.

Today, drinkers can once again gather for *l'heure verte*. If you take a seat at the bar in Boucherie, you can experience the tradition of the classic absinthe drip. This herbal spirit connects the absinthe drinkers of today with those in the buzzing bars of 1890s Paris.

3 TYPES OF ABSINTHE TO TRY

Boucherie has about a dozen types of absinthe stocked behind the bar; here are three of our favorites to try, recommended by Anthony Bohlinger.

* Jade Nouvelle (U.S.A) "This vert absinthe has a beautiful color with aromas of lemon balm and wormwood. There are subtle flavors of dark chocolate and a bright salinity."

* La Muse Verte (France) "A delicious French vert. It is one of my top picks for cocktails with great aromas of anise and good acidity."

* Tenneyson Royale (France) "A great blanche absinthe. It has Gin-like botanicals and is funky and rustic with flavors of pine, mulberry, juniper, and anise."

FRANCO MEXICAN WAR

Del Maguey Vida mezcal, Saint George Bruto Americano,
Suze, lime cordial

*"This refreshing cocktail combines French and Mexican
ingredients. I wanted to create a cocktail with 4
components: sweet, sour, bitter, and earthy. This drink is
smoky and sweet from the mezcal and lime cordial, bright
and bitter from the bruto, and earthy from the botanical
rich Suze. A crisp finish from the tonic."* -A.B.

**RECOMMENDED
READS**

Learn more about absinthe
and the craft of making
cocktails with a few of
Anthony's favorite reads.
These insightful books are
industry essentials:

A Taste of Absinthe
by R. Winston Guthrie and
James F. Thompson

If you want to experiment
with absinthe in cocktails at
home, pick up this insightful
book that covers the storied
history of absinthe and
features cocktail recipes
from some of the country's
top cocktail bars.

The Craft Cocktail Party
by Julie Reiner

Acclaimed New York City
bartender Julie Reiner
outlines everything you need
to know about seasonal
drinks, techniques for
creating outstanding drinks
at home, and how to
substitute spirits based on
what's already on your
shelf.

Cocktail Techniques
by Kazuo Uyeda

This book opens the door to
the unique world of
bartending in Japan.
Cocktail nerds will go
behind the scenes with a
Japanese master bartender
to learn about hospitality
and why the smallest details
matter in the best drinks.

INGREDIENTS *Serves 1*

1oz Vida mezcal
1oz War mix (1/2 oz Suze Saveur d'Autrefois
and 1/2 oz St. George Bruto Americano)
1oz Lime cordial
1/2oz Lime juice
Tonic topper

PREPARATION

1. In a tin add mezcal, war mix, lime cordial
and lime juice.

2. Shake hard for 7 seconds, fine strain into an
AP wine glass.

3. Fill glass with ice.

4. Top with tonic, garnish (skewered lime
wheel, pomegranate seeds and chamomile
buds) and serve with two small straws.

BOUCHERIE

www.boucherie.nyc